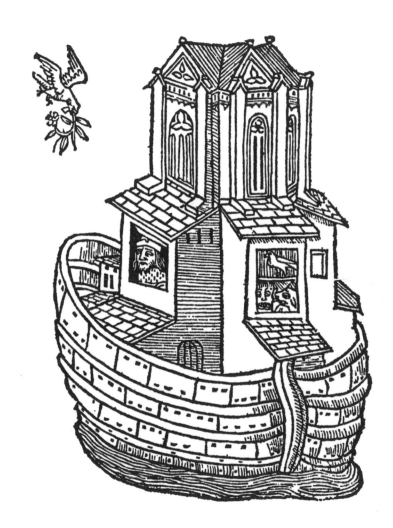

The dove returning to Noah's ark with the olive branch. Anonymous woodcut from the book *La Mer des Histoires* [The Ocean of Story], Paris, 1536.

SEASON'S
GREETINGS

The Madonna and Child in a Garden with Angels. Anonymous woodcut from the book
Gut nüczlich lere und underweysung [Good and Profitable Teaching and Instruction],
published by Johannes Bämler, Augsburg, 1476.

SEASON'S
GREETINGS

Festive procession. Anonymous woodcut from the book *Hystori von den siben weisen meystern* [Story of the Seven Wise Masters], published by Anton Sorg, Augsburg, 1480.

SEASON'S GREETINGS

Real and fanciful animals of the Middle East. Anonymous woodcut from the edition of
Breidenbach's *Reise nach dem Heiligen Land* [Journey to the Holy Land]
published by Anton Sorg, Augsburg, 1488.

SEASON'S
GREETINGS

"The Angels" by Walter Crane. From *A Book of Christmas Verse*,
selected by H. C. Beeching, 1895.

SEASON'S
GREETINGS

Angel. From a thirteenth-century stained glass window
in Lincoln Cathedral, England.

SEASON'S
GREETINGS

Cat. Woodcut from *The History of Four-footed Beasts*
by Edward Topsell, London, 1607.

SEASON'S
GREETINGS

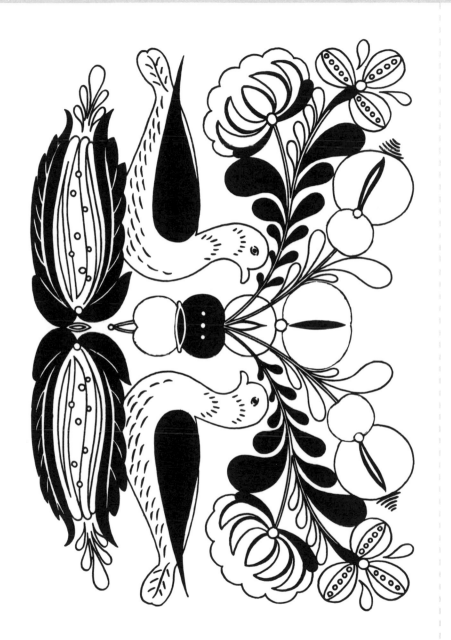

Design from a painted tin Pennsylvania Dutch cookie box, nineteenth century.

SEASON'S GREETINGS

Christmas toy from Marshall Field and Company's
Illustrated Catalogue, Chicago, 1891–92.

SEASON'S GREETINGS

Yule scenes by an anonymous artist.
From *St. Nicholas Magazine,* c. 1905.

SEASON'S
GREETINGS

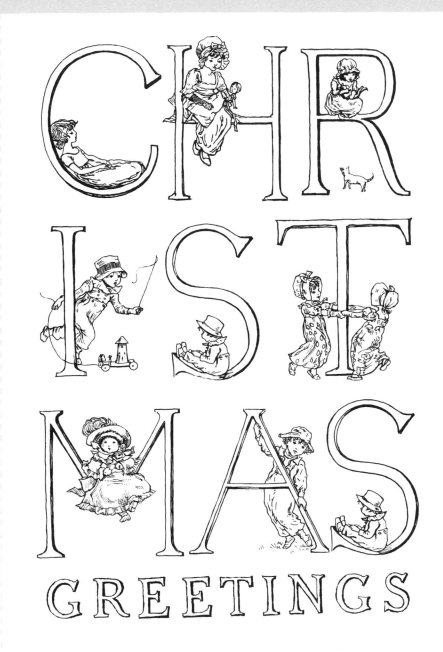

CHRISTMAS GREETINGS

Letters from a woodcut alphabet by Kate Greenaway, London, 1885.

AND A
HAPPY
NEW YEAR

A snowflake Christmas tree. The individual flakes are from
Cloud Crystals, A Snow Flake Album, collected and edited by "A Lady,"
and published by D. Appleton, New York, 1864.

SEASON'S
GREETINGS

"Merry Old Santa Claus" by Thomas Nast.
From *Harper's Weekly*, Jan. 1, 1881.

SEASON'S
GREETINGS

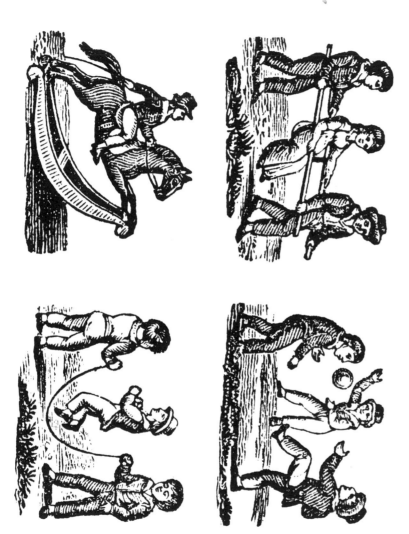

"Ride in a Chair," "Foot Ball," "Rocking Horse" and "Skipping the Rope." Anonymous woodcuts from *Juvenile Pastimes, In Verse,* an American book published about 1820.

SEASON'S GREETINGS

Woodcut initials from an early sixteenth-century
Romant de la Rose, France.

SEASON'S
GREETINGS

"Coaching" by William Nicholson.
From *An Almanac of twelve Sports*, 1898.

SEASON'S
GREETINGS